Simple Selling

ABOUT THE AUTHOR

Thomas Ray Crowel has been a salesman all his life. At ten years old, he sold hobby horses door-to-door that he made in the basement of his family's home. At twenty, his sales career began in earnest.

In 1965, he founded the Crowel Agency, Inc., which offers a wide variety of personal and commercial insurance. He started the agency from scratch, and, after a few rocky years, became very successful. Not content to rest "on his laurels," he continues to expand and diversify his business interests.

His entrepreneurial spirit has served him well. Although there were some failures, the successful companies he founded include an insurance agency, a finance company, an insurance training center and a franchise car wash.

He credits his knowledge and experience to the streets, the doorsteps and the sales interviews he has conducted throughout northern Indiana and Illinois. Tom graduated from Purdue University with a degree in clinical psychology at the age of forty. He did graduate work at the University of Chicago. Even with his education, he still believes the best classrooms are in the school of hard knocks.

He has been elected or appointed to numerous government and civic boards, and continues to serve whenever he is called.

Born and raised in Hammond, Indiana, Tom resides with his wife, Nancy, in nearby Highland, Indiana—the area known as the "region." This is where he intends to stay. He considers his accomplishments his legacy, and is forever grateful that both his sons have joined him in business.

He spends his time selling with his sons, Thomas Gehrig and Robert Ray, who are now partners. He enjoys reading, fishing and cigars—not necessarily in that order.

Simple $elling

Common Sense
That Guarantees
Your Success

by

Thomas Ray Crowel

Illustrations by
Louisa Matturro Boshardy

**$ Success
Press**

Success Press, Highland, IN 46322
© Copyright 1999 by Thomas Ray Crowel

All rights reserved under International and Pan-American Copyright Conventions.
Published in the United States by Success Press, Highland, IN 46322

Library of Congress Catalog Card Number: 99-60332

ISBN: Paper: 0-9669917-0-2
      Cloth: 0-9669917-1-0

Cataloging-in-publication data:
Crowel, Thomas.
Simple selling: common sense that guarantees your success/
Thomas Crowel.

p. cm.

ISBN: Paper: 0-9669917-0-2
      Cloth: 0-9669917-1-0

1. Selling—Handbooks, manuals, etc.   I. Title.

HF5438.25.C76 1997   658.85
                                                QBI96-40360

ACKNOWLEDGMENTS

Writing this book has been a labor of love. Over thirty years of selling has taught me that no one makes it in this business without the support and guidance of many others. I want to acknowledge those who have helped me through. In some small way, I want to return the dedication that so many have given me over the years.

In no particular order: My mother, Delphia E. Crowel, to whom I owe my curiosity for learning. My father, the late Otis D. Crowel, who instilled in me his work ethic, "never give up." My wife Nancy, for her dedication—she spent as much time raising our sons as I did making sales calls. My sons, who show me daily that they learned from my example.

My sister, Marjorie Crowel Wells, who continues to teach me the importance of family. My brother, Larry D. Crowel, my first teacher and business partner. Patricia Ann Gillham, my agency's general manager, who typed and retyped this manuscript and hammered out its contents with me for over two years. The late D.F. Bates, my first mentor. Yetta Matturro Wieland, who took my thoughts and words and edited them until they flowed. Her sense of humor made the editing process painless.

And last, but certainly not least, each and every one of my agency staff, whose dedication to minding the store enabled me to concentrate on this book.

For Patty
People think, machines don't

INTRODUCTION

People have bartered for goods and services since the beginning of human history. Much of the information I share in this book is not new. I hope, however, that I have presented it in a simple manner, one that will be a new perspective on a very old profession.

Information that can increase your knowledge and sharpen your selling skill is well worth the effort it takes to find. The selling process consists of many things, some of which can be taught, and some which can't. If you genuinely like talking (and listening) to people (are a people person) and believe your product fulfills a need in the market-place, you are more than halfway down the road to success. Another important characteristic goes by many names. Some people call it common sense, or horse sense or even mother wit.

In life, as well as sales, your common sense guides you to make the right decisions. But common sense makes sense only if you have the right information to guide you. In today's information world, knowledge is no longer optional; it is necessary.

My book is about you, the salesperson, and the many roles we play in today's marketplace. On any given day, we are both buyer and seller. In sales, the buyer and the seller change roles many times. You must be the judge of how my examples apply to your career.

I have kept this book simple for two reasons. First, many times we overlook the important things in life. We remember a name but forget what the person is about. Second, we all need to refresh our knowledge so we can stay on track.

For the already successful, seasoned salesperson, I do not intend to show you a different approach to selling. I do hope to remind you of what you already know. You can reflect on your road to success. Refresh yourself.

For those of you who are just beginning, or need a helping hand at selling, my humble advice is to treat your customer as you would like to be treated. Be fair with your customers. Your reward will be both personal and profitable.

This book is a primer for the rookie and a diary for the pro. Simple selling uses common sense. I hope you enjoy reading and using this book. Good Luck!

—Highland, Indiana, 1996

TABLE OF CONTENTS

SECTION 1

CHOOSING A
SALES CAREER

The chief business of the American people is business.

—Calvin Coolidge, Jan. 17, 1924

Why Sales?

So, you need a job, or were just offered one, and you want to find out if a career in sales is right for you. People choose a sales career for a variety of reasons. Whatever the reason, the most basic requirement, which can't be taught, is that you should be a "people person." Because a salesperson interacts with many people, you must like people to succeed. A good sale offers the thrill of a challenge, financial rewards, and, of course, pride in a job well done.

Salespeople interact with their customers. Although there are many similarities in people, there are also differences. This makes meeting new customers exciting. Your conversations vary daily. Selling is also a continual learning experience. I like that and so do most salespeople. Selling affords the opportunity to exchange ideas and knowledge. A sales career has an abundance of customers as well as colleagues.

A career in sales offers a challenge. The customers are a challenge. They demand the best quality for the least amount of money. Colleagues, on the other hand, offer competition. This is another type of challenge, and of course, good salespeople are always challenging and competing with each other. Setting new sales records, establishing goals, gaining accomplishments, and earning money are all a part of career selling.

Since everything is bought or sold, a sales career is financially rewarding. The only limits are those set by the salesperson. In many instances, the sky is the limit. Selling, therefore, is a high income career.

I saved one of the best reasons for last: when done honestly, the buyer, as well as the seller, profit. Both benefit. Both enhance their lifestyle. Both profit from the sale. There is always a sense of pride that a customer has after a purchase—for example: buying a car, a home, or any item that fulfills a need or provides comfort. Salespeople also share that sense with them, because both were part of the selling process.

Who Sells?

Everyone sells. Everything you can imagine is sold—even politics, religion and relationships.

Effective political campaigns are always in need of finances. Candidates and their supporters must sell the voters on the fact that their programs meet the public's needs. The candidate also has to convince the electorate that they can lead and serve. So, as you can see, winning an election and serving the public require the ability to sell yourself.

Religious leaders must also convince their congregations of their ability. The church needs money to exist and to operate their programs. In addition, the leaders of all religious groups sell their spiritual messages to their members.

Both business and personal relationships need salesmanship to be successful. Both need to find common ground. First, the individuals need to become familiar with each other and get to know one another's interests and preferences. Next, the ability to negotiate and compromise are required.

Whatever the relationship, negotiation and compromise are valuable tools. When you think about it, there's a little salesmanship in everyone.

Summary

Section 1: Choosing a Sales Career

A sales career offers:

- The challenge of selling your product and competing with your colleagues.
- Financial reward: in sales, the amount of money you make is based on your ability to sell your product.
- Pride in a job well done: Buyer and seller both benefit from the sale.

Everything is bought and sold. Proven sales techniques are used to sell everything—not only goods and services; but also ideas, concepts and ability. A good salesperson must like to talk, listen and learn from customers to be successful.

SECTION 2

PREPARING FOR
A SALES CAREER

*The people may be made to follow a
path of action, but they may not be
made to understand it.*

—Confucius

Appearance

Look your best. People do judge a book by its cover. The major reason that you want to have a great image is two-fold: first, it will enhance your sales; second, if you look good you feel good. A good attitude will also increase your sales.

People like to purchase products that appeal to them, and before salespeople attempt to sell their product, they must first sell themselves. To be successful, look successful. If the cover of the book doesn't get our attention, we usually won't open it. The same applies to food. If it doesn't look tasty, why taste it? Your appearance should give you the utmost confidence and then the customer will have confidence in you.

If you are well groomed, your attitude reflects it. A positive attitude is one of the greatest assets of a salesperson. Appearance contributes greatly toward attitude. For example, when high school students prepare for their senior prom, the young adults want to look their finest. It is an event that they want to remember for a very long time. They put on their gowns and tuxedos and want everything to be perfect. Many photographs are taken on the "big night," and the whole atmosphere is one of laughter and happiness—rightly so, since everyone feels good and their attitudes are positive. Everyone's mood is upbeat.

Salespeople need to be "up" to be effective. The way they present themselves is as important as how they present their product. A person's attire can be compared to a newly washed and polished automobile in that it brightens your outlook while driving.

Millions of dollars are spent by product designers to make their product appeal to the general public. Fashion designers spend big money to get the consumer in a buying mood, and runway models express an attitude of successful confidence.

Image is important. As a salesperson you don't have to spend a lot of money on your appearance; but you must invest enough so that you acquire a successful look to present to the public. You need an image that gives you confidence to secure the trust of your prospects and customers. People tend to do business with those who not only are successful but also look successful.

Political analysts claim that during the Nixon-Kennedy campaign one of the most influential factors that helped Jack Kennedy become president was the fact that he looked better than Richard Nixon on television during their debate. Looking good is one of the easiest things to accomplish. It's simply a matter of presenting yourself at your best.

It's not my intention to go into detail on how you should dress. There have been many books written on the subject. I would like to take a moment for you to consider how you feel on the subject of dress and grooming. Would you trust a banker if he looked as if he just finished cleaning his gutters? Would you want a doctor who looked as if he had slept in his clothes for a week? First impressions are very important. "Looking the part" is not only one of your easiest accomplishments—but also one of the most crucial.

Self Improvement

Self-improvement is always admired. People respect those who better themselves either personally or professionally. It takes discipline and effort to succeed.

Whether trying to lose a few pounds or studying to pass an examination, you must sacrifice. Eliminate the hours spent sleeping, and your time is divided between work and pleasure. Choices become difficult for many salespeople, that is, when to work at selling and when to take time off. Whoever was responsible for saying, "Work before pleasure" was right on target. Other than for a few rare individuals, the daily grind is not always pleasurable.

Once we agree that success takes effort, we can discuss the individual who either can't seem to get started or who finds other ways to put off the job of getting down to business. I find that if I jot down the things I would like to accomplish, I stay on track. Make a list of work goals and once completed, cross out those items that you've accomplished. Next, strike out the things that you would like to get out of the way. Finally, eliminate the not so important items but ones that will add a little extra bonus to your objectives. The list is complete. Don't make it difficult for yourself. If you don't get everything accomplished, then add the leftover items to the top of a new list. Learn to prioritize your time.

When people learn how to organize, they can accomplish a lot more in a smaller amount of time. I might add there is no sense in placing items on your list that you never intend on doing. Be honest with yourself.

Spend your work time working. No one says on their death bed, "Gee, I should have spent more time at the office."

Stay Informed

The quickest way that I know to get information is to seek it out. You can learn by listening, observing, reading, and doing. No matter what method a salesman decides to use to learn, he has to know the product he is selling.

I once had a job working in a garden center. I think I was about twenty years old. I knew next to nothing about grass seeds, fertilizer, lawnmowers, or any other equipment; however, most of the answers the customers were looking for were right there in the building. All of the various instructions were either on the packages or were explained in brochures. I spent much of my time reading about grass seed on the grass seed packages. The equipment was described in books or paper foldouts. I always read the material as if I were going to make the purchase. This way, I gave the products the detailed attention I would need to answer the customers' questions. If possible, it is always best to think in personal terms: how would you like to be assisted? The customer is served best this way.

When it comes to learning about products, most companies have their own training programs. Products, over time, change as do programs. Many products are updated, some are improved, and others are discontinued. To stay abreast of your product, you should know the competition and acquire a broad knowledge of your own industry. The knowledge is always available; however, the very best salespeople take advantage of information. Today, consumers are accustomed to reading and viewing data before they purchase. As sales representatives, we are expected to answer their questions and to make recommendations. This is only possible by knowing our products.

Accountability

Be responsible. It is hard sometimes to admit we make mistakes, especially ones made at work. However, when a new concept or a new approach to an old idea is taught, errors are bound to happen. If there's one thing wrong with fouling up, it's not admitting it. Ask anyone who has been in the position to train or teach someone, and they will agree that making excuses gets in the way of learning, for both student and teacher.

First, if you can't admit an error, it's very difficult to move on to something new. For example, if while driving a car you make a wrong turn, you would not get where you were headed. If you keep going in the wrong direction, it will take even longer to get to your destination. Until you admit that you made a mistake, your fate remains the same—you are lost and on the wrong course. To correct your mistake, you must stop and ask someone, look at a road map, or re-think your decision. Most decisions fall into this category. To correct an error, you must first be convinced that an error has been made. You either have to be shown the error or realize it yourself.

But how can you correct a mistake if you don't know what it is? I have made many mistakes while selling. One of the more embarrassing mistakes I made happened while selling an insurance policy to a fiftyish man and a twenty-something woman that I had presumed was his daughter. It was a very poor assumption. I asked, "Where's your wife?"

He told me the young woman was his wife, and I lost the sale. I always try not to take it personally. It gets in the way. Mistakes are made when the salesperson doesn't understand all aspects of what they are selling. Reselling is always harder than selling.

It is easier to teach people who admit they don't understand the material. It allows the teacher and student to work together toward a solution. A trainee has to be willing to learn.

Being willing to learn means being held accountable. Forget making excuses. Permit your instructor to train and teach. If you do this, you will find that the entire process becomes a lot simpler. Learning will also come quicker. After all, once you learn a procedure it will be your responsibility to share it with a new trainee somewhere down the line.

You never know when you will be called upon to share your knowledge. For example: artichokes were served at a dinner party. One of the guests, a physician, did not know how to extract the heart from the vegetable. The hostess showed him how to do it, and he proceeded to teach other guests. He exclaimed, "This is just like medical school, see one, do one, teach one."

Training

Since you cannot successfully sell by accident, it is important to know that you are receiving proper training. Most companies have training programs for their employees. They want their salespeople to know how to sell. It's also necessary for their salespeople to know about their product. Sales are of major importance to companies, and a well-trained sales force is necessary to reach their sales objectives.

Training can be provided in various ways. Some businesses send their salespeople to training schools. Others have them participate in correspondence courses. Many teach and train while they are on the job. This is usually accomplished by assigning an experienced salesperson to the trainee. The time and effort spent on training is determined by the product being sold. The more complex the product, the longer it takes to learn.

Whatever training method is used, it takes experience for the salesperson to become proficient. The best way I know to ensure success is through the selling experience. The more sales interviews you complete, the easier selling will become. The nice thing is that you learn from failing and succeeding.

The reason sales interviews are so important is that over time they build confidence and proficiency. For example, every hit a baseball player gets makes the next time at bat a little easier. Perfect practice makes perfect play. Each sales interview is an opportunity to practice selling. The more you practice, the better you become.

Summary

Section 2: Preparing for a Sales Career

- Salespeople need to be well-groomed and present a polished image to the public. Your image should not be flamboyant or sloppy, but one of successful confidence.

- Organization is a cornerstone of success. Make lists. Accomplish goals. Discipline yourself to keep your sales goals on track.

- Continue to update your knowledge of the product you sell, the competition, and the industry in general. Be aware of current trends both in sales and product development. Your customers expect you to address their concerns. Your product knowledge gives you an edge on success.

- Your career depends on your ability to learn from your mistakes. Admit your errors, learn from them, and move on.

Your experience will be called upon somewhere else down the line.

- Sales training is provided through various means. Some commonly used methods are training schools, correspondence courses and on the job experience. Don't get discouraged with the process—we learn from both failure and success.

SECTION 3

YOU'RE READY, GET SET...

Difficulty is the excuse history never accepts.

—Edward R. Murrow, 1959

Systems

If you think you can build a better mouse trap, do it. However, before you begin, make sure you know how to use the one that you presently own.

Everyone, including you and me, wants to improve on whatever system we use. The message is "keep it simple." Before you start changing and rearranging, you must have a general idea of how those things are supposed to work. For example, before I decide to try a different path, I want to know where the existing trail leads. If taking proven routes to particular places is the safest plan, then why do so many of us want to change successful sales systems before we fully understand them? We do it for two reasons: one, most of us like to contribute, and second is our desire for individualism. The first, contribution, can only be successfully accomplished by knowing how we are contributing. For instance, let's use the example of looking for a shortcut. In order to determine what part of the route to eliminate, we must first know the reason that the existing path was established. If the trail is well worn, then many before us have followed its course.

When the time comes to look for an alternate way, we must know what we seek. Discoveries have occurred by chance, but only a fool fails to take advantage of what is at hand. I always instruct sales trainees to use and copy what has been successful for their predecessors. Then, when they are comfortable with those sales methods and are at ease and successful themselves, they can make changes. Sharing ideas has always been handed down from salesperson to salesperson. Positive changes should be made from time to time; however, most sales concepts are basic. So, it's good to contribute, but resourceful salesmen and women first learn the basics.

Once a person becomes successful, sales methods are adjusted and changed. This benefits the sales process. Individualism in selling is necessary for self-fulfillment. Eventually, it becomes part of the selling system; therefore, it should forever be encouraged. For example, before a composer becomes proficient, he or she must study music. He or she must be able to distinguish between notes and chords, as well as other basic principles of music. Once the student learns the basics, he or she may decide to arrange music to individual preference. The same holds true for salespeople. Before they can arrange their sales presentations to their own satisfaction, they must first learn the basics. Then, with what they have learned, they will be able to add new ideas that contribute to the presentation or the closing of a sale.

Business Cards

One of my proudest moments when I began my career was the day I picked up my first business cards. A business card is something that you can hand to a potential customer when you introduce yourself. It can be an "ice breaker" as well as a reference card. It is and can be a conversation piece. An effective salesperson should always have one on hand.

When you present your business card, you are introducing who you are, where you are located, and how you can be contacted. Most business cards give a person a general idea of what it is that you are representing. The card is inexpensive. You are your best advertisement.

Since it allows you to briefly explain what your business or message is, your business card gives you those precious moments that are usually needed on first contact. The card assists you in beginning a conversation with a total stranger. It is a simple concept. The recipient of your card can decide to accept or reject it. Instantaneously, it gets the receiver's attention. It also gives people something to look at and consider while they are thinking of something to say. It's polite.

In addition to being a courteous conversation starter, your business card may be used as a future reference. The card is designed so a person can store it away for use at a later date. It gives the receiver that option. The business card is much more effective than a sales brochure. A sales pamphlet can assume too much. The sales piece attempts to sell. The business card introduces.

Even when not offered, I have had people ask for my card. Business people at times run out of them because they are so frequently requested. The simple business card is still the least expensive way to get your message out. Even after thirty years, it still gives me pleasure and a great amount of pride to offer my business card to someone. I believe that a salesperson should not be without one.

Practice

Practice makes perfect only if you practice properly and often. Ask anyone who is successful. Whatever you choose to do to become proficient, you must do it regularly.

Golf balls are hit over and over at the driving range for a number of years before a golfer becomes one of the best. Very few athletes have natural talent. I remember reading somewhere that if people would practice between five and six hours daily over a five year period that they would become successful at whatever they had set out to do. I don't believe that would hold true if they did not practice satisfactorily.

What I do know and am willing to share with you is that if you do not spend some time sharpening your sales skills, your chances of selling will decrease. Each time a salesperson has an interview with a client, there is an opportunity to learn. It's okay to make mistakes. When the golfer misses the ball, or strikes it improperly; he has the chance to repeat and correct his swing. The salesperson has the same chance and choice. He or she can correct what went wrong on the next try. Like any sports career, a career in sales takes time and practice to learn and many hours to perfect. The trick is getting started.

Loyalty Stands Out

If you find that you are unable to be loyal to a company or a product, it is time to leave. It is difficult to sell something in which you have no faith. Enthusiasm is a major part of a sale. Almost everyone knows that it is easier to be happy when you are actually happy. To act pleased takes more effort. A sale takes a lot of energy. A salesperson needs all the energy he or she can muster; anything that takes from that selling energy should be discarded.

If you work for a company that you think treats the public or yourself unfairly, then leave it. To stay would be dishonest to yourself and your employer. Next, being deceptive to the customer is improper. Finally, a salesperson should believe in the product he or she is selling.

I have always been fortunate. Over the years, I have sold only those products that I trust. My rule is simple—if given the opportunity I would purchase the product that I sell. Do not spend time learning all about a product only to find that you are not convinced of its need in the marketplace. Top salespeople must believe in what they are selling.

Remember, for you to convince the buyer to purchase your product, customer objections must be addressed. This can be difficult; almost impossible if you are not sold on the product. Loyalty and honesty go hand in hand. A salesperson needs both in order to succeed.

Commissions

Salespeople receive their income from any and every combination of salary, commissions, or benefits. When compensation includes commission, the obvious question is "What percentage of total sales will I be paid?" There is nothing wrong with asking, but there is more to consider than the amount.

You should evaluate how your product is competitively priced. If all other factors such as quality and service are equal but the marketplace won't tolerate the price, then commission wouldn't matter because the item won't sell. The same holds true for commission if the salesperson doesn't sell. After all, one hundred percent of nothing is still nothing. First, research the product you want to sell.

It takes time to get comfortable with anything new, so it's in your best interest to get familiar with your product instead of counting your commission before you've made a sale. Remember, the marketplace controls competitive pricing and the corporate structure must offer competitive commissions.

I have found it most profitable to first take care of what the customer needs. If done properly, income or commissions will follow. Legitimate companies realize that if their sales force is not compensated fairly, their sales will suffer and their salespeople will look elsewhere.

Getting Ahead

Honorably do what it takes for you to get ahead. Decide on a plan and follow it. Remember, nothing is written in stone. Be flexible. Be willing to make adjustments. Know changes are unavoidable; but by no means worry about what others are doing. To be more exact, never let jealousy get in your way. Jealousy is the most negative of traits. It's a waste of time and counter-productive.

When people spend too much time denying others their success, they have less time to succeed. How can people produce if they base their productivity on others? People are misdirected and mislead if they use their energy worrying about what they don't have rather than what they could have. There is nothing good to be said about jealousy. The only certainty is to avoid it.

Keeping Score

At sporting events, you can count on seeing a scoreboard. For instance, at most football games the scoreboard is near the end zone. The scoreboard functions include keeping track of each team's points and informs the coaches and players about the game such as time remaining, yardage, downs, etc.

Money is how we keep score in business. How much a salesperson makes is a good indication of how many sales he or she makes. Much like coaches and players reading a scoreboard, salespeople should keep track of the other factors that inform them about where they are in the "selling game."

It's best to have a simple system. This score sheet should include records of the interviews-to-sales ratio and the best times and days of the week to make sales calls. For example, I always found Mondays to be a good day to catch up on paperwork and to plan the rest of the week. Mondays are also a good day to regroup. Keep track. Purchase a sales planner to track your sales. If your record keeping is simple, it will take little effort to maintain. Sales planners can be purchased at office supply stores. Years ago, my boss told me that "A short pencil is better than a long memory." He was right!

Rainy Days

Pay the mortgage or rent that's due. Pay the car installment or transportation fares. Pay the utilities. Pay the telephone bill. Pay for groceries. Pay, pay, pay. When most people are finished paying, there is nothing left to save. Sales representatives need to know how to save. It is important because of selling cycles. Look at the product that's for sale, and you will usually find the selling cycle. For example, outdoor pools sell in the summer, and ski equipment sells in the winter.

If people are going to have any money put away for a "rainy day" or better yet a "nest egg" for sales slumps, they are going to have to find a way to save some money. It is not what you make, but what you are able to keep. A system to save is needed.

The trouble lies in how some folks "divvy up" their money once they receive it. Before paying everyone else first, put something away for yourself. Whatever you earn, a certain amount should be held in an account just for you. Determine a percentage, perhaps ten percent of each check that you receive. This amount will add up over time. Also, by putting some of your earnings away you are not just working for someone else. You are working for you! Once the first ten percent is deducted, then the remaining money can be used for expenses.

This sounds simple because it is simple. The hard part is staying committed to the amount once you decide. However, after you get started you will find that taking care of yourself first not only becomes easier, but makes more sense. Whatever system you find that suits your needs, stick with it. Remember, pay yourself first!

Summary

Section 3: You're ready, get set...

- Learn your company's sales technique thoroughly before altering any steps in the process. Once you have success with a proven plan, you may adjust your presentation to your own style.

- You are your best advertisement. When you offer your business card to potential customers, take the opportunity to talk about your product.

- Practice your presentation. Learn from your mistakes. Rome wasn't built in a day, and you will not likely be an instant success in sales.

- Leave a company or drop a product in which you have no faith. Dishonesty and deceptiveness are not endearing qualities either professionally or personally. Tom's rule of thumb: Don't sell a product you would not buy. Don't work for a company that isn't fair.

- When negotiating compensation, remember to consider your product's price, quality and service. If the customer is satisfied, commissions and referrals will follow.

- Jealousy is a waste of energy and counter productive. Don't deny others their success or worry about what you don't have. This energy is better used for your own advantage.

- Keep a record of your interview-to-sales ratio. Plan your day and keep track of your progress.

- Set aside money to pay yourself before you pay your bills. Selling has cycles which are unique to each product.

SECTION 4

MOTIVATION

*There is no security on this earth;
there is only opportunity.*
— Douglas MacArthur, 1955

Naysayers

Negativity is one of our worst enemies. It is an enemy because it always works against you. To succeed, you have to believe in yourself. If you are not convinced that you can succeed, you probably won't. Don't get me wrong; failure itself is not negative. How a person perceives failure is what counts. For example, one individual may say "I'm not going to make it." The "it" could be passing an exam, winning a race, finding a job, etc. Another person may believe the opposite. However, let's say for the sake of example that both individuals fail; the difference, and, I might add, a big difference, is in the person who at least gave himself a chance to succeed. It is said that failure is the other side of success. I believe it, and so do many successful individuals.

Saying "If at first you don't succeed, try, try again" is still effective. I would just add two things. First, before you try, think positive. Believe that you will succeed. Second, if you fail, by all means try again. However, re-evaluate your strategy so you don't follow the same path. Again, believe first in yourself, and second, never be afraid to change course. Anyone can tell you that you will succeed, but more importantly is, "Do you believe that you will succeed?" If you do, then chances are you will. It is extremely important to have a positive mental attitude. Success is born from dreams.

Be An Optimist

It's so easy to find fault in others. Look for the best in people. Find people's good attributes. Look for beauty in everyday events. This attitude is essential for success. It is the basic difference between the optimist and the pessimist—between success and failure.

The adage of the pessimist seeing the glass as half empty as opposed to the optimist seeing the glass as half full is a good example. A few years back, I was asked to speak at a sales conference. These speeches always center on motivation. Although joke telling is not one of my strong points, I did choose one that I heard years ago, and to be quite honest, it brought the point home. Here's how the story goes: There are two ten year-old twin brothers who are placed in separate rooms with one-way mirrors to be observed by a team of psychologists. One boy is always happy, the other is not, and the experiment was designed to find out why. In one room was placed every toy imaginable. The other room was filled with horse manure. Upon observing the boy in the room full of toys, the psychologists found him crying. When asked why he was so unhappy, he replied, "I have played with every toy in here, and I have nothing left to do." However, when checking on the boy in the room with all the manure, the psychologists found him to be whistling and shoveling along. One of the psychologists was amazed, so he asked the boy, "What on earth do you have to be so happy about?" The boy replied, "With all this horse s_ _t in here, there must be a pony somewhere!"

So there you have it. Some people will always look for the best, while others will not. If you are going to stand out in sales, you need to acquire the characteristics of the optimist.

People find ways to avoid the pessimist. All of us like to hear good news. It is easy to be an optimist. All you have to do is look for the best and keep a positive mental attitude.

Stay Motivated

Most salespeople find it hard to stay motivated. To be successful in sales, staying motivated is essential. Money, awards, prizes, and other recognition are methods many companies use to encourage salespeople to sell.

Money is always a motivator. Everyone is interested in additional income. Purchasing items to enhance your lifestyle takes funds. Recognition is also important. Many companies offer awards to recognize their top salespeople. Some companies sponsor contests with prizes for those who sell the most.

Whatever method you use, self motivation is important to your success. Accomplishment has always been important to me. I like to sell. I like the "high" that I get from closing a sale. Knowing that I have been instrumental in helping people make the correct decision gives me satisfaction.

To stay motivated is difficult. You must focus on the end result at all times. For example, if you want to keep in good physical condition, you must have a healthy regime such as jogging, lifting weights, or another activity that requires exercise. Some people find working out to be fun, while others find it sheer drudgery. For most, the result has to be satisfying to stay enthusiastic. The same thinking must be applied to selling. If salespeople are to stay motivated, they need to set goals.

These goals can be either short or long term; however, they must be achievable. For example, let's say you want to take a vacation and your destination is two thousand miles away. To drive two thousand miles at one time would be too much. If you set a short term goal of four hundred miles of driving per day, the total distance would be manageable and the goal achievable. Also, during your four hundred mile per day drive, I am quite sure you would even set even shorter goals. For instance, stopping for breakfast, lunch or dinner, plus "pit stops." For the same reason, goals are a necessity in selling.

A salesperson may have the long term goal of winning the "Sales Representative of the Year" Award; however, to have the award as a goal may seem too distant. If the salesperson thinks of the short term goal of so many sales per week or month, then he or she will stay more focused, and the "Sales Representative of the Year" will not be out of reach.

Luck or Hard Work?

"The harder I work, the luckier I get" is a quote I remember from the beginning of my selling career. It still holds true.

I have heard people refer to others as lucky. It's as if they are describing someone who just won the lottery. Successful people are usually thought of as lucky; however, in most cases it's just not so. The successful folks I have known over the years usually tell a success story of hard work. Remember that this so-called luck comes in two forms: good and bad. Bad luck is not often discussed. I would recommend that you think in terms of hard work rather than luck. For example, the performance of a successful athlete is the result of long years of hard work. In the music industry, an "overnight" success comes after years of playing in small towns. What you see is discipline, dedication, and sacrifice. That's what it takes to get the job done.

To succeed, you must have self-discipline. For a figure skater, this means practicing many hours a day, over a long period of time. The skater must be on the ice at 5 or 6 in the morning rather than sleeping late. Sacrifice is a word that is part of all success stories. The same can be said for the successful salesperson. You must do the things that it takes in order to be successful. Personal sacrifice is one of those things. To be a winner at what you choose to do, you must forget the term "luck," replace it with "work," and success will be yours.

Commitment

Keep your commitments. Making a goal or committing to one, does not mean you have reached that goal. If you want to succeed, you must be honest with yourself. Your goals have to be within your capabilities.

Never set yourself up for failure. For example, if you wanted to lose twenty pounds, it would be foolish to commit to losing twenty pounds in one week. It's more realistic to give yourself more time. This way, you could reach your goal.

You have a better chance at success if you set short-term goals. Set goals that will maintain your interest. After all, it is the achievement of short-term goals that make the long-term ones possible. A salesman who commits to making a certain number of sales calls each day has a better chance of reaching his goal than a salesman who promises himself so many sales per week. If you decide to contact five prospects a day, stick with it. Don't settle for less. If five turns out to be too many, then make an adjustment; however, a goal can be too small as well as too large. When it comes to selling there are really no limits—only the ones you place on yourself.

Looking for a Hook

Hooks are devices to hang various items on— things like coats and hats. When you look for an excuse, many times you are searching for someone or something to blame. You are looking for a "hook." This is negative. Negatives get in the way of success.

It is almost impossible to achieve while concentrating on failure, so why set yourself up? For example, on a windy afternoon at the ballpark, the baseball player tells himself that it is going to be difficult to hit the ball well because of the wind. He continues to concentrate on the wind. It will be hard to get any distance on the ball with a strong wind blowing against him. The wind will interfere. There's the hook. He has made an excuse for himself. It will be very difficult for him to f˗˗˗˗˗˗ on hitting. The wind is his "hook."

What about a "hook" for a saleswoman? She has been sitting in her office going over a list of prospects. Should she make some telephone calls? After a few moments, she decides that it will be hard to find anyone home. It's a week or two before Christmas. She surmises that everyone will be out shopping. She figures that even if they are home they have probably spent their money on presents. The "hook" has been created. The holidays are "out" for prospecting.

These are just a couple of examples of excuses people use to set themselves up for failure. The list could go on and on. The secret is to create positive situations. Take the baseball player, for example. The wind also will be a definite disadvantage for the opposing team's fielders and for the pitcher. The player should focus on success. The same is true for the saleswoman.

She should consider that during the holidays most people will be in good spirits. And, it will be easier to find someone home since many families have children on school break.

To be successful, think of success. Imagine the end result before it happens. The baseball player should visualize himself running toward first base after a hit. The saleswoman has to "see" herself setting up an interview and making a sale. Confidence and success go hand in hand. The mind is powerful. Top salespeople learn how to use this power to their advantage.

Summary

Section 4: Motivation

- Negativity is a salespersons worst enemy. Think positive. Believe that you will succeed. If you fail, try again.

- Be optimistic. Look for the best in people and keep a positive outlook.

- To stay motivated, focus on the goals you have set. Keep both short and long term goals attainable.

- Discipline, dedication and sacrifice are the attributes of "luck." Luck is the end result of hard work, and to be successful in sales, replace the word "luck" with "work."

- Set realistic, reachable goals. If what you want seems too distant or too vague, rework your goals into smaller, short term ones. Remember the example of weight loss; weekly goals are easier to reach than monthly goals.

- Don't set yourself up for failure. Visualize success and imagine yourself in the picture.

SECTION 5

PROSPECTING

We demand that big business give the people a square deal; in return, we must insist that when anyone engaged in big business honestly endeavors to do right he shall himself be given a square deal.

—Theodore Roosevelt, 1913

Numbers and Suspects

Selling is about the number of calls made and the quality of those calls. I call it "the numbers game."

First, you must find suspects. Next, convert them into prospects. Then hopefully, they will become sales. A sale is not possible without a prospect.

Let me first explain a suspect. A suspect is someone you don't know. He or she may (or may not) have a need, desire, or ability to pay for what you are offering. Suspects are basic to the sales process. A suspect is someone who may develop into a good prospect. The big difference between a suspect and a prospect is the suspect has not been qualified to meet the criteria to be considered a prospect. The salesperson doesn't know if there is a need or ability to pay. These are the two things that it takes to make a good prospect. Without suspects there will be no prospects. The prospect is the qualified suspect. The outcome is either a sale or no sale. From here, it's up to you.

It's not difficult to understand. If it takes twenty suspects to obtain ten prospects and from the ten prospects you close two sales, you can figure out your percentage of initial contact to closings as 10 percent. If you want more sales, then you must arrange more interviews. The bottom line is the more interviews a salesperson has, the more he will sell. To be successful in sales, you must be successful at prospecting.

The prospect's needs must be considered first. If the salesperson finds during the initial interview the suspect has no need for the product, then to pursue the sale is fruitless. For example, don't attempt to sell a car to someone who does not drive. The need must be established in order to have a bonafide prospect.

For some products, such as cars, insurance, home repair, etc., the suspect has to also meet additional requirements. If the suspect is under legal age to enter into a contract, then a sale would not be possible. The under age suspect does not make a good prospect if your product requires a contract.

The final obligation that a salesperson has to himself is to ascertain whether potential customers have the ability to pay. If the possibility of paying for the product is not feasible, then the suspect will not be a good prospect. Individuals may very well have a need and also qualify for a product; however, if they are unable to pay for the product, then they will not be a good prospect.

The surest way to find out if an individual qualifies as a prospect is to ask.

A short interview, asking the right questions, is needed. Only until a salesperson has a legitimate prospect does the entire sales process between buyer and seller begin to take place.

Need, Desire, and Ability to Pay

There are three important factors to consider while making a sale. First, there has to be a customer need, then the desire to purchase, and finally the ability to pay.

Customers should have a need for a product that you are attempting to sell. For example, they may find it necessary to own an automobile. However great the need, the desire must be there. In the example of the car, the need is apparent, but the customer may lack the desire to own one. The list of reasons could be long. They might have a fear of driving, or maybe they don't want the responsibility of ownership, or the cost of maintenance might discourage them. But let's say the first two considerations are satisfied in the customer's mind. They decide the need is there, and their desire is great enough to overcome any reluctance to buy the car. However, the ability to pay for the car is still a consideration.

They may not have the finances to make a monthly car payment or just don't have the required down payment.

I have used the car sale as an example, but you can apply these three factors to almost any sale. The salesperson must make sure the customer is making the right decision; otherwise, the sale is lost from the start or canceled somewhere down the line. Qualifying a customer is accomplished by careful interviewing on the part of the sales representative.

Prospecting Methods

Prospecting is one of the most important parts of the entire sales process. Without it, sales interviews and presentations never happen. There are many prospecting methods. Some of the most commonly used methods are telemarketing, door to door canvassing, and direct mail.

Telemarketing

There are a variety of companies that perform telemarketing duties for sales forces. Basically, they all work pretty much the same. They employ individuals who make telephone calls to residences or businesses that may be interested in a certain product. The reason telemarketers are so popular is because they make the initial sales call.

The first call establishes contact, and is usually the most difficult for salespeople. It "breaks the ice." During the first call, telemarketers collect data. They find out if the prospect is interested in the product and also if the product is appropriate for the prospect. Also, telemarketers attempt to discover what is important to the prospect.

When completed, the telemarketing company sends the information they collected to their customer. The information includes names, addresses, interests, years in business, and other data that salespeople can use when they make their contact. Depending on the type of product being sold, the telemarketers' function varies widely.

Some telemarketers only pre-qualify prospects for some products, while others set appointments and basically do a pre-sale.

Once the data is received by the sales force that requested the telemarketing service, it is up to them to determine how the information is used. The information supplied measures the level of interest. The salesperson will determine priorities. At this point the salesperson has identified hot, warm and cold leads. In other words who should be contacted first, second, etc. Once a decision is made on which ones might be interested in the product, the salesperson begins to make sales calls. The contacts are made either by telephone, mail, or in person.

During the first contact with the prospect, the salesperson refers to the telemarketer and relates the information he or she was given by the telemarketer. If properly done, telemarketing is effective and inexpensive.

Door-to-Door Canvassing

Going door-to-door attempting to set up sales interviews can send cold chills up and down the spine of many seasoned salespeople. However, if done with the proper attitude as well as the proper procedure, it's not all that frightening.

Since I had a number of successful years selling door-to-door, I'm going to share with you the attitude part first, which I believe is the most important part.

If you take rejection personally, I don't recommend door-to-door canvassing. Obviously, you are going to receive many refusals. After all, you don't have an appointment. You are taking a risk of interrupting someone. Since you are also gambling that the prospect is receptive to you and at times find just the opposite, you may encounter people with a disagreeable attitude. Therefore, it is imperative that your attitude is exceptional.

It sounds crazy, but I have found "cold" canvassing fun. It was like opening a box of Cracker Jack: I never knew what the prize would be; however, I always had hope that it would be a good one. Behind each door stood a challenge. Sometimes it was good news, and many times it was bad news. I never took it personally. I made many sales this way. Even if I didn't make a sale, I was able to introduce myself.

The introduction is the second part. The rule is this: never make a "cold" call without having something to place in the hand of the prospect. This item can be a business card or a small gift. For example, a list of emergency telephone numbers, or a small package of flower seeds works well. The best item is your business card. With it, you can state your name, company, product, and the rest depends on their response. To attempt anything other than a future appointment is usually futile.

Door-to-door canvassing is rarely done today. A majority of households now need two incomes to survive, therefore, there is no one home to canvass. In addition, there are many neighborhoods in which door-to-door canvassing would not be safe. Today, companies usually send direct mail to their prospects, and then follow up with phone calls.

Direct Mail

Sending information by mail is not only popular among companies, but is also done in large volume. The reason it's popular is because it is one of the easiest ways to make customer contact. It is a passive way to sell. Because it doesn't require an immediate response from the prospect, it is effective. To make the success rate of mailings greatly increase, many salespeople follow up with a telephone call.

When salespeople send one of their company's brochures through the mail, it usually includes a reply card. If prospects are interested, they request additional information, or file it away for future reference. Many times, a free service or gift is offered to prospects. Mailings can be very elaborate or kept simple. How they are presented has a lot to do with their effectiveness.

To be really effective, they have to be sent more than once. Usually, three or four mailings followed up with a telephone call will obtain the best success rate. A direct mail program which eventually leads to contact between the prospect and the salesperson is the goal.

The Right Time to Prospect

To be assured of a fair chance at prospecting, you need to choose the proper occasion. There are some times that are more favorable than others. Choose those periods that are most likely to bring success.

Times when people are most likely to be in the office or at home (depending on the product) are acceptable. Weekends, especially Sundays, are unacceptable. Sunday is a day that will receive negative reception for prospecting. I always discounted weekends in general for attempting to prospect or to set up sales interviews. People view Monday through Friday as business days.

Many salesmen eliminate Mondays for making sales calls. One reason is that most people have a busy schedule at the beginning of the week. Another reason is most sales create paperwork, and many salespeople like to use Mondays to catch up. It is also a good day to plan the week and make lists of possible sales calls. A top salesperson is well organized. Since it usually takes the best part of a day to do this, I believe that Monday is a good choice for most.

Other than choosing the proper day, the correct time is also important. Pick an hour that you are fairly certain that you are not interrupting the prospect. For example, lunch and dinner time are out. If you pick either one of these periods to set up interviews, you will have a difficult time. These times may be fine for selling but are definitely out for prospecting. Since lunch and dinner times vary from family to family, you will need to allow an extra hour or so to accommodate for the differences. Many people are tuned in to their favorite television programs in the evening. Most individuals are aware of what is considered prime time. This should not be a problem for salespeople. Allow for special programs such as elections, major sporting events, and other favored times. Prospecting is not the easiest part of sales, it takes good judgment and a lot of consideration to be successful.

Quality vs. Quantity of Time

How much time you spend is not the same as how the time is spent. What's important is how your time is managed.

Time can be wasted away unintentionally. Most of us, at some time or another, have set out to do something only to be distracted. Maybe a friend stops by just when you are beginning a project, so instead of an hour spent on whatever you started to do, you end up with a total of three hours. Maybe you sit down to write an overdue letter and because of numerous telephone interruptions the letter takes five times as long as it should. You are still using time, but, you are not using it to your advantage; therefore, in order to get the most out of time you must plan carefully.

Another good example of outside distractions is a radio or television set turned on while you are reading difficult material. As you read the words, you don't pay attention to their meaning. When you're finished with a paragraph, you have to go back and read it again because it didn't make any sense. You were looking at words but missing their message.

If you are planning on spending one hour each day telephoning your prospects, then you have to be sure that the hour is used wisely. Before you start your calling, all the names and telephone numbers must be organized and set out before you. You have to be free from interruptions; otherwise, the time you planned for prospecting will be reduced because of outside interference.

In the business of selling, it is too easy to put off getting started. Without concentration, the typical salesperson finds himself or herself wasting valuable time. At the end of the day, he or she is surprised that no time has been spent at all in accomplishing what was set out to do. Use time so it counts.

Forget how many hours have been spent prospecting or selling. Instead, make certain the time spent is quality time.

Supermarkets

The next time you enter a supermarket, I want you to think about corn. That's right: corn. The grocer makes his living selling cans of corn (and, of course, lots of other things).

Now the grocer would not let himself run out of corn; if he ran out, people wouldn't shop there. For the grocer, the corn is his "stock in trade." Without it (and the other things that bring customers into his store) he is out of business—as surely as if his store had burned to ashes.

As a salesperson, your "stock in trade" is your prospect list. When the grocer runs out of corn, he has nothing left to sell. When you cross off the last name on your prospect list, you have no one left to sell to.

The successful grocer always has the corn ready for his customers. When the grocer's corn shelf runs low, he fills the empty place with new cans.

Your prospect list should be like the grocer's shelf: always full, always fresh and always current. The grocer can't sell from an empty shelf. You can't sell from an empty prospect list.

Contributing

Sometimes an interview goes smoothly and results in a quick and easy sale. We leave the interview wondering what we did that was different from the interview before. We promise to do exactly the same thing the next time. But, did we really do anything different?

Sometimes we interview a prospect and do everything "by the book." We answer objections, try to close, answer more objections, try again to close—and the prospect doesn't buy. Did we do something wrong? Where did we make a mistake?

We may not be aware of it, but the easy sale may have been ours because another salesperson had paved the way for us. That salesperson may have put the prospect in the mood to buy. For one reason or another, the prospect didn't buy. When it was our turn, the pre-selling done by the other salesperson made our job easier.

And it may happen that we are the first to interview the prospect. We may set the stage for the close, and, in effect, pave the way for the next salesperson.

Even though we may compete for the same customers, we help each other—sometimes without the knowledge of doing so. Medical students (and doctors) have a way to say it: "see one, do one, teach one." We learn from our colleagues and, at the same time, we instruct them.

Another Look at Prospecting

Think of a prospector panning for gold, and it will be apparent how salespeople seek out prospects.

If you and I wanted to strike it rich prospecting, the first thing we would do is find a probable place for gold deposits. We would need to do some research, look at geological surveys and study accessibility. Once we located an area where we would most likely discover gold, we would need to make a strike.

Prospecting for potential customers is much the same. The salesperson must look where the

chance of finding success is the greatest. For example, it would be best if you are selling watercraft to find prospects near water. If you sell garden plants, you must prospect in late winter.

The first issue is always need. The prospect must have a need for the product. Like the gold prospector, the salesperson must constantly prospect to stay successful.

Searching for prospects is an ongoing process. It must be done regularly. If you don't prospect, you will be out of business. The best system is the one that works for you. There are sales seminars and books to help you stay motivated. You can network—contact those you know in similar areas of sales and share ideas about locating prospects. The system you use needs to be compatible with three things: first, the time you are able to spend, second, the effort you are willing to put forth, and third, the way you keep records.

Time spent prospecting is time well spent. Without prospecting, there would be no leads, no interviews and no sales. How you spend your time is important. Time can be visualized in two ways.

Just spending time prospecting isn't effective. For example, a salesperson sitting at his or her desk for hours on end shuffling leads without deciding who to call is not effective. The cards become worn and dog-eared from constant rearranging. Can't you just picture the gold prospector sitting all day, looking at the mountains, trying to decide which one has gold? He sits and wastes his time thinking about where to begin.

It's more effective to use your time wisely. The gold prospector selects a mountain, chooses a spot, lifts up his pick and shovel, then begins digging. The salesperson must do the same. Pick up the phone and "dig in"—call potential prospects. This way your time is spent more economically. Many salespeople find this difficult when it should be simple. Decide how many sales calls you want to make and then complete them. However, time and effort alone does not work unless you keep track of your effort.

A successful salesperson keeps a record of time spent prospecting. Just as the gold prospector needs to keep track of where he has dug for gold, the salesperson needs to keep a record of results. By keeping an index card file on your prospects, you will be able to record the time and date of your calls. You will also have room for notes.

Record the time and date so that you can establish when your prospects are available. There is no reason to call each day at one o'clock if that's the lunch hour. Always note the time and day that you made contact. A "no answer" or "busy signal" is not a genuine sales call, but it should be noted on the prospect's index card.

By jotting down remarks, you accomplish a couple of things. A brief statement reminds you of the best time to make contact. It also reminds you what was said. For example, the prospect advised the salesperson to call back in two months only to have the salesperson call back in two weeks. This type of error can and should be avoided. All it takes is a brief statement on the index card.

Time spent prospecting is one of the most challenging aspects of sales. At times, it is tedious, discouraging, and difficult. However, without it there are no sales. As with most things in life, the end result, getting paid, is something that many of us look forward to. I can honestly say I have always made the very best of prospecting. You can too.

Customer Participation

It is very important not to do the majority of the talking during a sales interview. Two reasons come to mind. First, the salesperson will not become aware of the customer's needs, and second, you will lose the customer's attention. To succeed in closing sales, the customer needs to be able to speak out, and the salesperson needs to listen up.

The best way I have found to get the customer involved in the sale is to ask questions and wait for the answer. Don't stack questions on top of questions. One questions at a time can be challenging enough. Many times a single question involves a lengthy answer.

Frequently, customer responses uncover objections. Only by listening will you be able to respond. When looking to buy, most people want to be sold; give them a chance to be heard.

Most of us, when lectured, will eventually become bored or inattentive. You've probably heard the term "windbag," or someone described as full of "hot air." A successful sales presentation needs discussion. It requires the customer's input. The customer has to be a part of the sale. The only way he can participate is by voicing his opinions, objections, and preferences. Unless you ask, you will never know what customers are thinking. A customer must have his "say so." Therefore, listen and learn. Avoid talking yourself out of a sale.

Summary

Section 5: Prospecting

- Suspects are basic to the sales process. First they must be found, converted into prospects and then, hopefully, they will become sales. The best way to find out if suspects can become prospects is to ask. Does this person have the need, desire and ability to pay for your product? If so, the suspect is now a prospect, and the sales process between the buyer and the seller can take place.

- Qualify your prospects through careful interviewing.

- Prospecting is an ongoing process. Some of the most common methods of prospecting include telemarketing, door to door canvassing, and direct mail. See text for definitions and advantages of each method.

- Choose the right day and time for prospecting. Depending on the product you are selling, certain times of the day are inappropriate. Tom's rule: Never prospect on the weekend.

- Don't waste time getting started. Organize your prospect list, be free from interruptions, and pick up the phone. Jump right in.

- Be sure your prospect list is always fresh and current, just like the grocer's shelf. Don't let yourself run out of prospects.

- Salespeople contribute to each other's success, even without knowing they have. Sometimes an "easy sale" can be attributed to another salesperson's efforts— sometimes your presentation will make the sale easier for the next salesperson.

- Time spent prospecting is time well spent. If you don't prospect, you will soon be out of business. Keep records of your prospecting efforts. It is tedious, discouraging and difficult; but without prospecting, there are no sales.

- Don't lecture your customers. Let them participate in the sales presentation by asking questions, voicing their opinions, and telling you their preferences. Listen and learn from your customers. If you don't, you may just talk yourself out of a sale.

SECTION 6

SELLING:
THE PROCESS—
BUYER CONCERNS

No one has a finer command of language than the person who keeps his mouth shut.

—Sam Rayburn, 1978

Paying Attention

Being a good listener is not easy. Like most people, I fall into that category. Hearing something that's being said and listening to what's being said are two different things. For instance, you may hear sounds coming from your TV but be totally unaware of the message. On the other hand, if you are listening carefully, you have a better chance of understanding.

A salesperson who listens to customers has a much better chance of closing a sale than one who does most of the talking. First, if you don't pay attention to what the customers are telling you, you will have no idea what questions they have or what answers they need.

It sounds simple: listen and learn. As simple as it may seem, not listening and talking too much are common shortcomings among salespeople. They are inclined to do most of the talking because they want the customer to be confident that they know what

they are talking about. This makes some sense; however, salespeople will never be fully aware of what their customer needs until they listen.

To be a good listener, you have to concentrate. You must listen like you think. Concentrate on one thought at a time or listen to each word so the entire conversation makes sense. This will take practice. Listening is not always easy. There's fear of forgetting an important part of the sale. This can be corrected by taking a few notes during the sales presentation.

Who Makes the Decisions?

How do you find out who has the purchasing power? You must ask. If you are selling to a business partnership or a marriage partnership, it's vital to know who makes the buying decision. Sometimes it is only one individual, and other times it may be a combination of people. The only way you will ever know is to ask your customer who should be included in your sales presentation. Another way would be to suggest that any and all parties who will be affected by the purchase should be included.

If an individual is excluded from the sales process and that person is the one who has the final decision, the sale is usually lost. At best, the sales person has to make the presentation over. This is not very cost effective. When one of the decision makers is left out, the sale has additional resistance. A good salesperson will find ways to eliminate wasted meetings. Sometimes it is impossible to include everyone; however, it is imperative to include the decision makers.

If, for any reason, a decision maker has been overlooked, find out why. If they are unavailable, delay the interview until they can be included, or until the customer assures you that all interested parties are present. It is impossible to close a sale if there is a hidden objector who has final approval of the sale.

Staying Focused

Once you find out what the customer needs, stay focused. From time to time, customers will question you to find the best price or best value. That's why it is so important to be a good listener.

Listen carefully during your conversation—customers will let you know exactly what they want. If you are paying close attention, they will also let you know how much money they want to spend. It is useless to attempt to sell someone something that they are not willing to pay for.

When the price range has been decided, negotiate within those boundaries. Otherwise, the sale is usually lost. In general, buyers know what they want. They have basic requirements to be met. Affordability is one of them. Although price is important, there are other things to consider such as quality and quantity. It's important to know when you are selling too little or too much. Again, you can only know this by discussing their needs. Their preferences are important.

If individuals are set on a certain color, then it would be a disservice to them to attempt to change their minds. Why try to change a customer's mind? It is much more fair to meet their requirements. When you know your customer and also know your product, it is easy to stay on track.

Chameleons Know When to Change

Chameleons change color to protect themselves. They accomplish this instantaneously by internal or external stimuli. Change is also a skill which salespeople need. First, accommodate the customer. Next, stay in control of the sale. Alert salespeople know when the customer is changing the direction of the sale.

Top salespeople are able to stay in sync with the customer's needs. They realize the importance of being understood by the prospect. It is not always easy. Many sales are lost by an inattentive salesperson. A prospect must be able to understand your presentation. Questions and objections have to be recognized and addressed.

Consider the customer who has just entered the hat department of the local store. She walks over to the shelves lined with various styles and colors of hats. The salesman strolls over and asks if he may be of service. The lady replies, "No, I am just looking." The salesman at this point has two obvious choices. One, to remain at her side while she looks, or the other is to say, "If you need help, I'll be right over there." Chances are if you stay, she won't. No one wants to be pressured. At this time, you don't know if the shopper is buying or looking. She looks in the direction of where you wisely decided to go. Once again the choices are there for the salesman. He can stay put or go over to the customer to assist.

The lady is holding a red hat in her hand. She asks the salesman if he has the same style in blue. Now, the salesman needs to make a few decisions. For example, does this customer want to be reassured that the red hat looks good on her, or does she in fact want to purchase the blue one? Most buyers are just like you and me. They look for input. Sometimes they like to get another opinion. You ask if she likes the hat's style or whether she is looking to match the color. A light bulb seems to go off in her head. "The red one will be perfect. It will match what I plan to wear this weekend. I'll take it," she says. If a sale was easy, it's usually because the interaction between the buyer and seller was harmonious.

It is the salesperson's obligation to see to it that harmony exists. The change in a sales presentation should be originated by the salesperson. Understanding and satisfying the customer takes sharp listening skills. The salesperson must be in tune with the prospect. Be like the chameleon: know when to change. Often the salesperson must shift from talking to listening. A top salesperson looks for customer signals. Listen and look for indications. Many times customers will direct you. It is no deep psychological secret. It is common sense and a matter of paying attention.

Chasing Rainbows

To keep trying to sell someone who has no intention of buying from you is useless. Most people, at some time or another, will buy something. However, this doesn't mean that they will buy from you. As the old saying goes, "You have to know when to get off a dead horse." Individuals make purchases for different reasons. I believe these reasons have a lot to do with their mood or timing.

As for mood, you might have a taste for ice cream one day, and the next day it's the last thing on your mind. It's like taking a walk, going to a movie, watching television, or an activity: you have to be in the mood. The same holds true for buying something. For example, one minute you feel like you just have to have an item, and the next minute you'll not be the least interested. Many sales have fallen through with the statement, "I'll be back later."

Since mood affects buyers, one could say that timing does also. Using the example of taking a walk, you may be in the mood but due to bad weather, it's not the right time. The same thing could happen going to the movies. You would like to see a movie that has just been released, but you don't have the money until next week. It's a timing thing.

I'm sure there are numerous reasons why people buy. Being in the buying mood and at the right time are two important things a salesperson should consider. Let's not forget another reason, "you." I'm sure you've heard the comment, "There's something I just don't like about him." If you read the chapter on "Five to Seven No's," and still don't get the sale, maybe you should stop chasing this particular rainbow.

Keeping on Track

During a sales interview, be sure to answer one question at a time. It is a mistake to drift from question to question. You will confuse the customer.

A customer asks questions because he doesn't understand. Questions must always be answered to the customer's satisfaction. You may need to use several examples. I always feel that customers have a good understanding of the information if they can explain it to me.

When you answer questions, pay close attention to the customer. Does he look like he understands what you're saying? If necessary, break the question down into smaller parts—take the customer through each section and answer one step at a time. If you think the customer doesn't understand, ask questions differently about the same topic. Your customer understands the presentation when he is able to "give it back" to you.

After all, an interview is about uncovering and answering customer concerns.

If the customer has several questions, write them down on a piece of paper. Then, answer them one at a time until the customer is satisfied. In order to close a sale, all objections have to be resolved. Another possibility is to tell the client that after the sales presentation you will respond to questions. However you decide to address the issue of answering questions, agree before the interview begins. The customer should be involved in the entire sales process to insure success.

Summary

Section 6: Selling: The Process—
Buyer Concerns

- Listen to your customer and learn his concerns. The only way to accomplish this is to listen closely and take notes if you must.

- Before you make your sales presentation, be sure you know who has the authority to make the buying decision. Include that person in the presentation.

- Stay focused on customer needs. If you pay attention to their concerns, you will know what they are willing to buy. Negotiate within those boundaries.

- Stay in control of the sale. Know when to "back off" and let the customer decide. Common sense and people skill will tell you when your input is needed.

- Sometimes it happens that the customer will not buy from you. It may be a personality clash or the wrong time in his pay cycle, or his mood.
- Answer customer concerns to his complete satisfaction. Ask him to "give it back to you" to make sure he understood the presentation.

SECTION 7

SELLING:
THE PROCESS—
SELLER CONCERNS

It is best not to swap horses while crossing the river.

—Abraham Lincoln, June 9, 1864

Gift of Gab

Why is it that many people believe that successful salespeople have a "gift of gab?" Or is it a good line of b.s.? What's alarming is that a few salespeople believe this to be true. It always seems to be music to the salesman's ear to hear someone say he could sell a refrigerator to an Eskimo. It's as if a glib tongue is a badge of honor or at least the "tool" of the profession. Here's the disagreement—I tend to think of selling as a learned skill. What is needed the most for successful selling is knowledge.

First, the salesperson must have product knowledge. To sell something to someone you must know what you are selling. This is one of the easier tasks for a salesperson to resolve. All that is needed is effort to learn all aspects of the product. This isn't asking too much.

Next, the salesperson should concentrate on the customer's needs rather than his or her own. I find it

disappointing to observe a salesman adding up his commission before the sale. It's too self-centered. If there is a rule, it should be this: satisfy customer needs and the commissions will follow.

Finally, to bring the point home, a smart salesperson knows when to stop talking. For salespeople sometimes it's a Catch-22—they can't shut up to sell and can't sell if they don't shut up. Listening is one of the most difficult things to learn. That's why we have two ears and only one mouth—listen twice as much as you talk. Most people have to learn how to listen. It takes patience.

Think First, Sell Last

Before you conduct a sales presentation, make certain you are prepared. Have all your bases covered. It is helpful to exchange ideas with colleagues. Good sales tips are always welcomed; however, like flying an airplane by yourself, you are alone. Before you call on your customer, spend some time preparing yourself—preferably alone.

Once you are by yourself, be sure that you have everything necessary for the sales interview. Many times, simple items are forgotten: things such as pens, paper, calculators, business cards, sales information, brochures, and applications. I know of sales interviews where the salesman even forgot where he was supposed to meet his customer. You need to be alone to prepare.

When you are off by yourself, you will have the necessary time to visualize the sales interview from beginning to end. Think over the general questions that pop up during a presentation. Go over all the dates, names, and possible references involved. Make certain your sales materials are up to date. All pilots review a pre-flight checklist. The same is true for alert salespeople. If you don't have a checklist written down, at least have one in your mind.

Be on time! Be prepared! If a salesperson does not know his product, if he is not prepared for the customer, or if he is not at his best, he might as well not show up.

Don't Sell What You Don't Have

Have you ever had a salesperson sell you on a particular item only to find out it is not available? The customer is disappointed, and the salesperson probably lost the sale.

Make certain you know what the customer wants. When in the market for a car, there are cer tain features or accessories that a buyer has in mind. For example, he wants four doors vs. two doors, or air conditioning, or a six cylinder vs. an eight cylinder, or a certain color and so on. The salesperson should find out in the first interview what options the customer wants and cannot be negotiated.

Once a salesperson is aware of what the customer desires, he or she should attempt to meet their expectations. It is a big mistake to "sell" a customer on a product that is no longer available. For example, you have decided to buy a new suit. After finding a suit you like, the salesman suggests a blue shirt to coordinate. However, after checking his stock, the salesman finds that your size is not available. He suggests a different color. Do you buy? Probably not, because he already sold you on the fact that the blue shirt was the best choice with the original suit. Check first for availability before offering something for sale.

When selling, offering choices or options is effective since you are including the customer. Many times I have encountered salespeople who have "hard sold" me on a product only to apologize later because it's no longer in stock. They usually attempt to "un-sell" you or sell you a second choice. However, once the error has been made it almost always means the sale is lost. So, be careful when you say, "I have just what you are looking for."

The Butcher

I once read an article about how butcher shops operate. It described how hamburger should be weighed on the butcher's scales. For example, if the customer orders two pounds of ground beef, it is better to underestimate the amount of meat before it is placed on the scale than to overestimate. The point being that buyers would much rather see hamburger added to their purchase than taken away. During a transaction, if people feel they are

losing instead of gaining, they feel slighted. It's human nature.

The same analogy holds true for most sales. If the salesperson offers something to the buyer, but is unable to deliver it, then the customer feels deceived—even if the item or feature of the product was not considered in the cost. That's why top salespeople check out not only the cost of their product, but make sure of its availability. Many times products change features and options. It is always best to know the product you are selling. Sales presentations should not illustrate discontinued items. Salespeople must be aware of what is available to the customers. Sales are lost over minor discrepancies.

Remember, buyers are looking for more for their money, not less. Successful salespeople represent that which is available. Once an option is "sold" as part of the product and then you discover it has been discontinued, it becomes very difficult to convince the customer he is getting a good buy. He feels he is losing some of the "ground beef" that he already bought.

Too Pushy

Being pushy isn't good. But be assertive. Most people have an idea of what they want to buy. They also know how they like to be treated.

I believe that a sales interview can be compared to a comedian telling a funny story. It can be repeated too often. Make sure you cover all the selling points that you believe are important to explain the product in detail. Also, answer, all questions that the customer has. Once you do this, the decision to purchase is up to the customer. If you have thoroughly explained the product and the customer clearly understands, the interview is over. Not every interview turns into a sale immediately.

Many times the customers need time to think. They want to be alone so that they can go over the information they received during the sales presentation. Once they are satisfied that they can use and afford the item you present, they will come to a decision. The only thing left for them to decide is if you are the salesperson that they want to buy from.

They will need time to make their decision. If the salesperson continues to repeat the same thing over and over, customers begin to feel pressured. If customers begin to believe that the salesperson's commission is more important than their needs, sales are lost. However, if buyers are convinced of the seller's honesty and their need is established, then a sale is likely; that is, if it is the right time.

Be Patient

Selling takes time. Most sales are not made on the spot. During a sale, a relationship develops between the buyer and the seller. The more expensive the product is, the more time it takes to sell. The process is always the same: the need and the ability to purchase. However, the larger the investment, the more buyers want to know. They want less room for error in their judgment. They correctly take less of a chance.

There is less risk in purchasing a one dollar lottery ticket than purchasing a thousand dollars worth of stock. People need the time to think about a purchase. Salespeople need to learn to give them that time.

Once you have given the customer the information about the product and have answered all of the questions, then it's time to wait for their decision. If you push, many times you will lose the sale. What's the rush?

Most people can anticipate when a salesman becomes anxious. They start to doubt the product. They begin wondering why the salesman is pressuring them. The customer starts to feel that the salesman's main concern is money. When this happens, the sale is usually lost.

If you keep a good list of potential buyers on hand, there is no need to lose a sale because of undue pressure. Let the sale develop. Let the customer feel comfortable.

Pick One

First, find out what the customer requires. Next, choose what he requests. Finally, stay with his choice. Many times the salesperson is trying to sell his own choices rather than conforming to the customer's needs. Get to know your customers by asking a lot of questions. Wait for the answers. If you do this, you will have a pretty good idea of your customer's desires.

When you are certain that all the customer's requirements have been met and are satisfied that he is aware of all the product options, it's time to focus on the product that will meet all the customer's criteria. Once the customer decides on a choice, stick with it!

Sales have been lost because of a "fickle" salesperson. Individuals want to make certain that they are doing the right thing. Sometimes customers will become distracted from the buying decision. They may do this to test the integrity of the salesperson. Other times they hesitate to convince themselves that they are making the correct choice.

A salesperson who stands firm and stays on target has a much better chance of closing the sale.

The guide, or rule, for all salespeople is to be confident about the sale once the choice is agreed upon. To do otherwise usually means a lost sale.

Collecting Money

What is the best way to request payment? Ask for it. Many salespeople never finalize a sale because they are too timid to ask for payment.

When I was selling door-to-door, I always gave the customers a choice. They could pay me with cash or check, but the choice was always to receive payment. I can remember back when I had to train salesmen. The choice was not always to pay. Sometimes the trainee would give the option of paying now or later. Unfortunately, sometimes later never came.

There is no reason not to ask customers to pay for the product. They expect it. After all, they bought it. It is the way our economy works.

When you do not ask customers for payment, you may give the impression that it's not worth the price. After all, everyone is willing to pay for a bargain.

A professional salesperson would never ask for payment until every question is answered to the customer's satisfaction. The customer must understand exactly what he or she bought. Anything less is shaky business.

Not Sold

A sale is not consummated until all parties involved have agreed and are bound by some sort of consideration. In most cases, the consideration is money. Having someone sign the "bottom line" does not always constitute a sale.

I have heard many salesmen say, "You can count this one sold," only later to discover that for some reason or another the sale fell apart. In many cases, the buyer had unanswered questions or could not afford the purchase.

If the customer's concerns are left unattended, the sale is headed for failure. Just because you feel that the sale is "in the bag" doesn't necessarily make it so. Once the buyer is alone, he has lots of time to reconsider what took place at the presentation. He will again think about what was said. He needs to be certain that he made the right decision. Tell the customer that you are aware that doubts may surface later. Advise the customer that questions will turn up once you leave; however, tell them to write them down.

Many times a sale will not happen until several interviews with the buyer take place. The more complicated and more expensive the product, the more selling time is involved so be careful about "counting your chickens before they are hatched."

Fish Stories

"All fishermen are liars." After all, what's a few pounds or inches added to a fish when a good story is at stake? In most cases, no harm is done. On the other hand, being untruthful about a product is quite a different story.

Exaggerating or bending the truth in sales is damaging both to the buyer and the seller. It's damaging to the customers because they may not be getting what they bargained for. Lying is disastrous for salespeople; it ruins reputations. The salesperson's word establishes that person as a professional. A good reputation will follow you. So will a bad one.

Sell the product for what it is. Offer it on its own merits. Add nothing. People understand that profit is included in the price. The public understands you usually get what you pay for. If you lie, you'll be discovered. Today's consumer is more knowledgeable. The media has made us more knowledgeable and informed consumers. For an honest salesperson, that makes selling easier.

Fear of Rejection

At some point or another, most salespeople fear rejection. The word "No" has a powerful effect. It's a word that brings terror to the salesperson's mind. Rejection is what gives even the best salespeople cold feet.

Remember back when you wanted to ask someone to dance at a school function and would not ask for fear of being refused? Or you did and the answer was "No." It took the wind out of your sails; plus, you just knew that everyone at the dance was watching and listening when you were rejected. Let's face it: rejection causes emotions to surface. One's self-esteem is on the line. Relax. Rejection does not need to be the same experience in selling.

It can be difficult, but always keep in your mind that you are not being rejected; it's the product, or the concept. For example, the customer may not like a number of things about your product—the color, style, shape, or conditions to name a few. And, let's not forget, of course, the price. Do not jump to conclusions. There are a number of things to blame for losing the sale. To be successful you have to overcome the panic that rejection brings, although it's healthy to be a little nervous.

One of the best ways to avoid having your ego crushed is to step back. Take a good look at what's going on between the buyer and yourself. It's the product that's on the line, not you.

Salespeople tend to think that the product is being sold because of them rather than by them. Some salespeople seldom give a thought to the fact that the buyer may or may not have a need or the ability to purchase their product. Keep this in mind. The salesperson is never more significant than the product. The successful salesperson's primary task is to present the product.

The Close

You have already read about many of the skills I believe will make your sales career a success. Throughout these chapters, I have discussed many elements of a successful close. The close is exactly what it says—the end of the selling process—when the sale is final.

The sales process is similar to a rehearsal; much effort is put forth before the performance. When the curtain is raised, you have only one chance to succeed. It's the same with a sales close. You get only one chance, so use every ounce of your knowledge and experience.

Make certain you skillfully explain your product, answer all questions and concerns, arrange for payment and know when to stop selling. There are many ways to ask for the sale. You might say: "What do you think?" "How does this sound?" "Do you have any more questions?" "Will you be paying by cash, check or credit?" Once you obtain a positive response, complete your paperwork. Say goodbye.

Closing a sale is so important that some organizations employ individuals to "wrap up" (or close) a sale. For example, after the sales rep makes the "deal" with you for an automobile, you are sent to another office to arrange your "paperwork." This is the place where payment is discussed.

Although some companies have the luxury of a special department or individual for closings, most sales are completed by the same person who does the prospecting and interviewing. Therefore, you must know how to close.

There are many methods that can be used to close a sale, and for experienced sales people the end of the sales process is second nature. If you are a pro at closing, then the following will be just a review, but if you're just beginning, read the next section carefully. You may know these different ways to close by other names. But, to paraphrase Shakespeare, a rose is a rose...

Ways to Close A Sale:

1). **The assumptive close:** You have addressed all of your customer's objections, but have not heard a firm "I'll buy it!" You ask, "Will you be paying by cash, check or credit?" Your question assumes the customer wants your product and will respond with an answer that closes the sale.

2). **If/then close:** Example: you are selling a used car. Your customer is hesitating because the tape player doesn't work. You can tell he really would like to buy the car, so you propose an if/then statement. "If I replace the tape player, will you then buy the car?"

3). **The when close:** Your customer realizes the benefit and believes your product to be superior to the one he currently uses. However, he still has many similar items in stock. Before he can say to call him back in month or two, you ask for the order. "Would you like this product shipped in thirty or sixty days?"

4). **The close as a method to discover hidden objections:** This is also a way to tell you when to stop selling. "What do you think?" "How does this sound?" Let the customer talk about any underlying concerns he may have about the product.

5). **The close as a method to discover buying authority:** For example, you are selling cleaning supplies and have been meeting with the head of maintenance. He likes your product, and can see that it would be a real time saver for him. When you ask for the order however, he tells you that he doesn't have the authority to make the purchase, and that the plant superintendent is the one who signs all his purchase orders. Although you may be frustrated at the moment, having spent all morning trying to sell this man, stop for a moment and think. Ask to set up an interview or ask to call back. This strategy often works. You have, in effect, the head of maintenance pre-selling your product to the plant superintendent.

The best sales reps are the best closers. If you want a successful career, the bottom line is: complete the sale.

Summary

Section 7: Selling: The Process—Seller Concerns

- You must know your product. Concentrate on customer needs rather than your own need of commission. Know when to stop talking, and give the customer a chance to say his piece. Tom's number one rule: If you satisfy your customer's needs; commissions will follow.

- Have a checklist of items you need for your sales presentation. Use it each and every time you make an appointment with a customer. Have up-to-date sales materials. Be prepared. Know your product.

- Find out what the customer wants, and make sure it's available before you offer to sell it to him.

- If you offer a product to a buyer, but are unable to deliver, the customer feels deceived. Products change and features change. Check for availability and cost.

- Don't try to "hard sell." Explain the important features of your product in detail and answer all of your customer's questions. Give him time to consider the purchase. Don't pressure him to buy.

- Selling takes time. The more expensive the product, the more time it takes to sell. Keep a current list of potential customers, so there is no need to lose a sale because of pressure.

- Don't try to sell your customer what you want him to have—sell him what he wants. Meet the customer's requirements; inform him of your product's options and stay with his choice.

- When the sale is final, ask for payment. The customer bought your product, he expects to pay.

- A sale is not finished until all parties have agreed and are bound by a consideration (usually money). Don't count a sale as "sold" until all these criteria are met.
- Don't exaggerate or bend the truth about your product. Offer your product on its own merits.
- Rejection is a necessary aspect of selling. A product cannot be all things to all people. Remember that it is the product being rejected and not you. In other words—don't take it personally.
- There are many ways to close a sale. You must be familiar with most. (Imitate the best; memorize the rest.) The best salespeople are the best closers.

SECTION 8

WISDOM...

Each success only buys an admission ticket to a more difficult problem.

—Henry Kissinger, March, 1979

Five to Seven "Noes"

Most of us have gone shopping for an automobile. When visiting the dealer's lot, we always start by looking at many cars.

When a salesperson spots a customer, he or she usually asks to be of assistance. The general answer he or she gets is, "No thanks, I'm just looking." Although I have used the car lot as an example, I could have used any shop or business. The first response to the car salesperson is a general response in almost all sales. I think of it as the first "No."

Following the first rejection, a salesperson can expect five to seven more. Customer resistance is a part of the sales process. Sales presentations and uncovering customers' objections, answering questions, and satisfying customers' needs are all part of the salesperson's obligation. Remember, very few sales are made without customer resistance. I believe that customers don't buy, but want to be sold.

Failure

It is said that failure is just another step toward success. Failure is no more permanent than success. In fact, that's what they have in common: neither one is constant. In order for a child to learn how to walk, he must fall. For a successful politician to win votes, she must know what loses votes. To be a successful salesperson, you must be aware of what won't sell. Just because your first attempt is unsuccessful, it doesn't necessarily mean the sale is lost.

Most people, including myself, want to be sold. Very seldom does someone walk onto a car lot, approach the car dealer, and say "Sell me an automobile." Usually, the salesperson will ask the prospective buyer if she has any particular questions about the car she is looking at. In many instances, the salesperson will ask if the prospect would like to take the car for a drive. Almost always the first answer the prospective car buyer will give is, "I'm just looking." When prospects state that they are just looking, they are buying time to come up with additional questions or objections for the salesperson. Very few individuals want to buy right away. Most of us want to be sold.

If the first step in a sale is usually failure, then what is the next step? The next step is usually failure too. In fact, most sales have at least five to seven "Noes" or "Not interesteds" before they become successful. Remember this, before a sale is final, prospects must have all objections answered to their satisfaction. Even after that, the sale is not always final. Most buyers have second thoughts.

If failure is the beginning of success, then what is the end? The end is satisfaction. Customers must be satisfied that they need the product or service. They must be able to afford it. Finally, they have to be sold on you so you can sell them.

If you attempt to sell someone something that they have no use for or they can't afford, your sales career will most likely not be a prosperous one. If you have high pressured a client into purchasing an item or service he or she is unable to keep or use, then you can be assured that you will not receive many recommendations or referrals. Customer satisfaction is not just a part of sales; it is what makes sales successful.

Hidden Agendas

No one wants to be kept in the dark. A hidden agenda is an unfair way of conducting business. It causes anxiety, suspicion, and other negative feelings.

It may make good conversation to talk about the expensive restaurant that has a menu without prices, and maybe there are a few people who are not concerned. However, there are a lot more folks that want to know exactly how much things cost.

In the past, people were always reluctant to ask their doctor how much a medical procedure cost. If they did, the answer was, "Let's not worry about that; let's just think about getting well." Times have changed. We can all be thankful for some of the changes, especially when it comes to eliminating hidden agendas.

When selling, if you tell your customer at the beginning the approximate cost of the product, a lot of unnecessary buyer anxiety is relieved. That relief produces more time for the customer to learn about your product. In fact, if your product costs more than a potential customer can afford, the sales interview will be unproductive.

One of the major points to cover when qualifying a customer is cost. People know what they can or cannot afford. I always become a little suspicious when inquiring about price only to have a salesperson tell me, "Don't worry about it; I'll cover that later." All through the sales presentation, I wonder how much the product will set me back.

After the Sale

Once a sale is closed, ask customers for referrals. They can give you names of friends, relatives, or business associates. These are the very best leads. For various reasons, many salespeople don't ask for them.

Salespeople may not request a referral from the just completed sale because they are so excited that they want to leave. It could be that the sale was difficult, and the customer asked many questions. Maybe salespeople figure that they could call back later and ask for a referral. It's hard to say why referrals are overlooked.

Remember to ask. The customers are the best source. They bought from you; therefore, it's much easier for you to call on a friend, relative, or business associate of theirs than to make sales calls on the telemarketing list of strangers. Usually, friends and relatives have a lot in common. Also, a referral implies trust and confidence in what you're selling—as well as in you.

The only way to obtain leads from your sale is to ask. Is there someone that they know who might be interested in your product (or service)? When individuals make a good purchase, they like to share their experience with others. It is human nature. There are two very good reasons to ask for referrals: first, it won't cost you anything to ask; second, a career in selling depends on prospects.

Service

The farther you go in sales, the more you learn about customer service. You will find that there is a wide range of opinion about what it means to "service the client." Since I believe that service is as important as the sale, I am going to share with you what has worked for me.

Service is what takes place before, during, and after the sale. Whatever you sold must now be delivered. In many instances, the speed of delivery is not your responsibility alone. You may depend on others in your company to prepare and deliver your customers' products. Don't make promises that you can't keep. Disappointing the customer immediately after the sale can only lead to bad public relations for your product.

Your goal is a satisfied customer. Remember, salespeople survive on references. A satisfied customer will result in referrals. Since just about everything is competitively sold, it is a smart salesperson who gives outstanding service. Think of the billions of dollars that companies spend on television commercials. With this in mind, ask yourself how service fits into the picture.

Providing service is imperative if you like your job and want to stay in business. Some methods of service are complex and technical. One, however, is simple. Never take a customer for granted. A salesperson should remain as available after a sale as before the sale. Take phone calls.

Customers don't expect a salesperson to know everything, although they are entitled to have their questions answered. Many times finding a solution to a problem or answering a customer inquiry takes time. Often, this occurs with no further profit for the salesperson. However, to acquire and maintain customers, the importance of outstanding service is undisputed. Successful salespeople make every effort to satisfy the customer. To do otherwise makes for a short sales career.

Half a Loaf

It's been said that a half loaf of bread is better than none at all. It's also true about sharing sales or commissions. Professional services are many times shared. The main object to remember is that the customer is the one who should benefit the most.

If a physician confers about a patient's health with a colleague or a specialist, it should benefit the patient. If the patient gains, then the business of fee splitting is positive. However, if it is done for the sole purpose of making money (and gouging the customer), then it is not only unethical but unlawful as well.

The same holds true for professional salespeople who are asked by one of their colleagues to share a product. Perhaps it's a product that they are out of, or one that they can't get in stock. If it helps customers to obtain what they need, then sharing the sale is well founded.

But remember, once a sale is shared, the commission is usually shared. Most of the time customers are unaware of the details since they usually deal with only one salesperson. It is simpler.

It is usually to the customers' advantage to negotiate with one individual. This way they know exactly who will be held accountable. No one likes to get the run around or be caught in a pass-the-buck situation. Sharing products or product knowledge is beneficial to customers because they get added service. Also, additional opinions are helpful, and they might expand your market.

Team Selling

The sale of a complex and expensive product or service may require a group effort. Very few salespeople have the range of skill needed to present the product and respond effectively to all possible objections.

Take the example of a company investigating the purchase of a million-dollar machine tool. The engineers must be satisfied that the machine is capable of producing the products for which it is being purchased. The manufacturing group must agree that the products can be produced in sufficient quantities in a reasonable amount of time. Maintenance personnel must be satisfied that the equipment is reliable and easy to repair.

And there's more—the financial group within the prospect's company have to determine that the purchase is affordable and will contribute to the company's profits. Last, and perhaps most important, the president and board of directors have to agree that the purchase conforms to the long-term goals and strategic plan established to insure the company's growth, competitiveness and profitability.

Now, consider your role in this example: if you have a technical background, you'd be comfortable with the engineers and the "nuts and bolts" part of the sales presentation. But would you be at ease explaining return on investment to the customer's accounting department?

Are you sufficiently familiar with the customer's competitors to explain to the president how this purchase will give him an advantage in price, service or quality?

Few of us are prepared to be responsive in all these areas. We are, however, able to use the resources available to us. Experts in all these areas are available. We can, and should, use them.

Every team has a captain. As a salesperson, you are the captain of the team. Your responsibility is to coordinate, motivate and lead your team. Done properly, the prospect's questions will be answered, objections responded to and the sale will be one step closer to completion.

Summary

Section 8: Wisdom...

- Expect buyers to resist. Expect to hear "no" at least five times. Tom's advice: Buyers don't buy, but want to be sold.

- Failure is not constant. It is forever changing. It is the beginning of success. Customers must need your product or service; they must be able to afford it; and they have to want you to sell it to them.

- Tell your customer how much the product costs. Don't keep him in the dark about price. It will save you time and effort if you find out up front that he can't afford to do business with you.

- Ask for referrals. Many salespeople neglect this important aspect of selling. Referrals from satisfied customers are the very best leads.

- Service takes place before, during and after the sale. Disappointing the customer after the sale leads to bad public relations for your product. Your goal is a satisfied customer.

- Shared sales result in shared commission. It can be beneficial to the customer because he can receive added options and service. Shared sales can benefit you by expanding your market.

- Team selling is a fact of life if your product is technically complex or offers multiple services. Remember, as the salesperson, you are the captain of the team.

SECTION 9

...And More Wisdom

*If you don't stand for something, you
will stand for anything.*

—Ginger Rogers, June 18, 1978

Who Do I Talk To?

Most of us have attempted to purchase a product or inquire about a service but have been unable to make contact with the salesperson. Many times, a relatively simple inquiry turns into a stressful event. Much of this can be avoided if you remember that most individuals are just like yourself. When you are looking for help or information you would like to connect with someone who can offer advice. You would like to talk to a person.

Telephone answering machines and voice mail serve their purpose, but one must realize that they only give instructions and not answers to questions. A telephone busy signal is the same as no contact. Being placed on hold too long creates a negative attitude in even the most patient. Finally, a broken appointment or showing up late does the same thing—and then some. It rearranges or ruins the day.

If you choose to make a career out of selling, it is necessary to be available to your clients and keep your commitments. Make yourself accessible. People like to keep in touch with those who are helping or advising them. Things that seem simple or minor to you can be very frustrating for a customer who has a problem they'd like solved. If you follow-up and handle simple requests, problems will not develop into major conflicts. Generally speaking, it is the small details and minor adjustments that make the difference between mediocrity and excellence.

Getting Up for the Sale

When an entertainer performs, he must be at his very best. If he's not, he deprives his fans of his true talent. Most performers have experienced being not quite up-to-par. Behind the stage curtain, they had to decide whether to cancel or to go on stage. If they decide to perform, then the audience must not know anything is amiss. That's show business.

A salesperson is like an entertainer. He or she must either perform or cancel. Sometimes, canceling is the only option. The appointment will have to be re-scheduled. If the appointment must be kept, then the salesperson must do his or her best. That means no shortcuts and no excuses. Customers deserve the full presentation. They should be treated as if nothing is the matter. Sales are closed on customer needs, not because of sympathy for the salesperson.

The needs of the customer should never be overlooked. After all, the price remains the same regardless of how the salesperson performs. Buyers, as well as fans of the entertainer, deserve their money's worth. Give the presentation your very best. It is not always easy, but it is the fair thing to do. After all, you could have canceled.

Jargon

Use language the customer understands. Every occupation has its own jargon. When the common abbreviation EKG (electrocardiogram) is used by medical personnel, it's okay. Everyone understands. However, there are many industry specific terms that are not common. Make sure you are understood in your sales presentation. Avoid jargon. Your sale may depend on it.

Don't use slang, either. I have had people talk to me in slang only to be confused by it. People don't always like to admit that they don't understand. It's human nature. To be safe, speak in simple terms. If you have ever listened to knowledgeable computer experts carrying on a conversation, I'm sure you know what I am saying; they use terms that are foreign to most.

Say what you have to say in clear, concise, well known words. Make sure that your customer gives you positive feedback. Only then do you know that you are getting your idea or message across. Save jargon for communicating with your colleagues.

Don't Try to Sell Over the Phone

Since you're reading this book, I presume you want to sharpen your selling skills. Let's take a minute to define what you are, what you do and how you do it. At the same time, let's look at what you're not:

YOU	TELEPHONE SOLICITOR
Initiate prospect interest	
qualify prospect	sometimes
Schedule face to face meeting	rarely
Explain product	
service at meeting	rarely
Respond to objections	sometimes
Close sale/receive payment	rarely
Service customer after the sale	rarely

Telephone sales (telemarketing) are a necessary part of business. Sometimes they are a company's principal method of bringing a product or service to the public.

We will not address telemarketing do's and don'ts in this book. The example above is given to make an important point: you can't sell over the phone, so don't try!

Your customers can't sign an order form over the phone. Neither can they write a check or pay with cash. In fact, you can't even be sure to whom you are talking—or whether they are qualified to make a purchasing decision.

Follow these tips for the best results on the telephone:

DO	DON'T
Prospect and qualify	Present the product
Set appointments	Attempt to close the sale

DO	DON'T
Service after the sale	Answer product-related questions
Ask for referrals	
Say, "Thank you"	

Remember that regular follow-up should be part of your sales process; phone follow-up is a good time to ask for referrals, too. Most importantly, remember to thank the customer for buying from you.

Glitz and Glamour

I once attended a political seminar that covered political campaigning. The speaker was addressing some of the do's and don'ts for candidates running for public office. One point that struck me was the topic of being too controversial. The reason I was so interested in the subject was because it is one that I have been aware of from the beginning of my sales career.

One of the first things that I was taught during my first training session was there is no reason to become involved in controversial subjects while selling. Many people's loyalties run deep when it comes to religion, politics, or organizations. Sometimes the slightest matter will trigger a full blown argument or discussion. Items such as emblems, rings, pins, decals, bumper stickers, and other items that could appear controversial should not be displayed by salespeople. They serve no purpose in the sales process.

By avoiding such items, I never felt I was concealing or hiding my convictions or beliefs, but was instead focusing on the business at hand. That is, doing the best job that I could selling my product. Most salespeople would agree that at times it is hard enough to stay on track, let alone open an entirely new agenda of questions and answers not pertaining to the product.

General conversation, or "small talk," does have a place in a sales presentation. Talk about the weather and other non-controversial subjects. More serious topics I discuss with close friends and family. The sales presentation is the main point. Do not become sidetracked.

When You're Wrong, Admit It

If an error has been made in cost, description, service, or ability of a product, the salesperson should admit it, even if it costs him the sale. Hopefully, when mistakes are made, they are either due to a misunderstanding between the seller and the buyer, or are totally unintentional.

Many times an error in price is made because the customer changed from one option to another. For example, when a salesperson is adding up the cost of the various features or choices, they will sometimes give the wrong final price. If this is done, admit it. Carpenters have a saying: "Measure twice, cut once." In sales you should calculate twice, quote once. By no means try to cover the mistake by placing the blame on the customer's misunderstanding. This will result in an argument, a lost sale, and a lost customer.

Sales can be lost in other ways. Too often, a salesman will make promises that he knows he can't keep. If he does it knowingly, his career will not last very long. Making a promise to a customer unknowingly might not be as blatant; however, it can usually be avoided by checking first. It is always best not to guess. You'll be on solid ground if you admit to the customer that you're not certain, and will check to find the correct answer. There is nothing wrong with not being an expert on everything. Honest mistakes happen. Admit your mistakes.

Problem Solver

Somewhere along the line, you will have a misunderstanding with a customer. Many things can and do get in the way of a smooth exchange. Delayed or incorrect paperwork, being late for an appointment, or a miscommunication are some examples. There are times when problems have no connection with the sale. However, it's better when you remember to be a problem solver and not a problem giver. Let me explain.

When people become upset over something, the one thing they don't need is to be further aggravated. I compare an argument to a fire: the more fuel tossed on a fire, the hotter it gets. So if you begin to argue with customers who need help, all you can accomplish is to get them more upset. Instead of this unsuccessful approach, I have found that the best thing to do is listen. Yes, listen to what they are trying to say to you. Make sure that you understand what's upsetting them. Then work to help solve their problem. You will find this approach works best.

Congratulations

When you read your local newspaper, certain sections contain items such as birth announcements, marriages, promotions, elections, and other articles on accomplishments. If there's a picture or an article of one of your customers, cut it out and send it with a card of congratulations. It could even be someone who's business you want. Most people like to be recognized.

If you want to get someone's attention, ask their opinion about something. When you mention the nice article or picture you saw in the newspaper, they will be pleased. In turn, they might mention it to their family and friends. If you never sell one thing to anyone that you sent an acknowledgment to, it won't matter. It doesn't cost anything to be nice. Additionally, the more well known you become in your community, the easier it will be to do business there. It's the thought that will be remembered.

Fine Tuning

Everyone has fine tuned a radio. Why listen to static or a station fading in and out? You carefully and gently turn the dial until you find the exact point where the sound is best. That's also how successful people operate. They fine tune things and events. For example, when a business transaction is complete, they let the customer know they appreciate the sale by simply saying "Thank you," or by telling the client how much they enjoy the opportunity to service the customer's account.

Think about this for a moment. We all like to feel appreciated. Isn't it strange that good manners are either missed completely or taken for granted? How many times have you bought something and heard the clerk say, "There you go!"

handing you your purchase? If you haven't, then the next time you go shopping just listen. You won't be surprised when you aren't even thanked by the sales clerk. I get the feeling that some sales clerks are as unhappy about taking my money as I am about spending it.

If you fine tune your sales mannerisms, you'll find that you will be more effective. It is the small adjustments that make the large differences. Please make this one of your selling habits.

Unfair Competition

Degrading your competition in any way is unacceptable, and it makes you look bad. Rather than talk about your competition, it's best to say nothing at all. To recognize a competitor by name is acceptable. To "knock" a competitor or his product is useless and unprofessional.

There is no point finding fault with your competition; your customer doesn't expect you to sell their product. Sell your own product; it is challenging enough. Attempting to answer questions about a product that you are not familiar with only adds more customer objections to your sales interview.

Most salespeople find that if they can explain their product, answer all questions relative to the sale, and present their product professionally, they have done a good job. Doing those three things doesn't necessarily mean a sale, but it does result in the customer's respect.

Salespeople need that respect in order to receive not only the sale, but also future referrals or leads. Without prospects, the professional salesperson cannot survive. Professionalism is admired by all.

Don't Hold Grudges

If you lose a sale to a competitor or a colleague—benefit from the loss. By no means hold a grudge. Always leave the door open for future contacts.

Sometimes sales are lost because your competitor has an advantage. Maybe their service is quicker, or the product costs less. Perhaps the competition is better known. You may never know why you lost that sale.

Over the years, I have lost sales only to get them back later. Some sales are just lost. It doesn't matter. The main thing to remember is to let go and move on. It is okay to review what went wrong, this is how we learn. To dwell on a lost sale is a waste of time. The next sale you have could be the one your competition lost.

Many times a customer will learn about a product from one salesman only to purchase it from someone else. Many of us educate ourselves at the expense of others. "Brain picking" is a part of the sales process. It works to salespeople's advantage as well as disadvantage.

There are many steps on the road from prospect to sales interview where the sale could be lost.

If the salesperson who lost can't get over it, the chances of future failure increase. On the other hand, smart salespeople know to accept loss because somewhere down the line success will come. That's the way it is: both win and lose.

Oversell

If you have ever been hunting, or are at least familiar with the sport, you know that once the game is dead there is no reason on earth to continue to shoot at it. However, if you did, it would be overkill.

When customers are ready to buy and everything has been explained to their satisfaction, they are prepared to close the deal. Once they have asked how much money they need to pay and have offered to pay it, but instead of accepting, you continue to talk and sell, you have committed oversell.

Some salespeople are unable to take "No" for an answer. Others are unable to take "Yes." Both types continue talking for some reason. Perhaps they want to satisfy their egos or to impress people with their knowledge. I assure you that whatever the reason, it's a mistake. When you oversell, you risk talking yourself out of the sale. It's always best to listen. By listening you will know exactly where you are in a sales interview.

Summary

Section 9: ...And More Wisdom

- Be reachable. Take phone calls. When a customer has a problem or a question, he usually wants to talk to a person, not a machine.

- A salesperson must not make excuses or take shortcuts when preparing or presenting a sales presentation.

- Don't use jargon or slang when discussing your product with your customer. Save jargon for talking with your colleagues. Using slang will "turn off" most customers.

- The phone is an important tool in sales. Use the phone to set up appointments, do follow-up and ask for referrals. Don't use the phone for selling. Customers can't sign an order form over the phone, and you can't be sure that the person you're talking to has the authority to buy.

- Don't give the appearance of being controversial. Items such as rings, pins, decals and bumper stickers could trigger a conflict with your customer. These items serve no purpose in the sales process.
- If you have made a mistake while quoting a price or discussing options, admit your error. Honest mistakes happen.
- Many things get in the way of a smooth exchange between buyer and seller. When problems occur, take care not to further aggravate your customer. Be a problem solver; not a problem giver.
- If you run across an article about or a picture of one of your customers in the local paper, clip it out a send it to him. Acknowledge those you know or would like to do business with in your community. It doesn't cost anything to be nice.

- Work on your sales manners—you will become more effective in your dealings with customers.
- Don't knock your competitor or his product when you sell. Your customer will have more respect for you and your product if you stick to the business at hand—selling your product.
- Sometimes sales are lost. Review what went wrong, learn from it, and move on. Don't dwell on lost sales.
- Don't oversell your product. Know when to stop talking. Be able to take "yes" for an answer.

SECTION 10

TWENTIETH CENTURY AND BEYOND

Our true nationality is mankind.

—H.G. Wells, 1920

Disappearing Services

Since the 1960s, many services have diminished. True full service gas stations no longer exist. It wasn't unusual for the attendant to ask if you would like your battery, oil, and tires checked. When your battery needed water, your engine needed oil, or your tires needed air, you never had to leave your car. The attendant took care of it for you. Cleaning the windshield was automatic.

When you went to the movies, an usher showed you to your seat by holding a flashlight, so you wouldn't stumble in the dark. I not only remember these forgotten services, I provided them. I worked as a gas station attendant, and as an usher in a movie theater.

What do air gauges and flashlights have to do with today? Increased sales and additional income. It's agreed that times have changed. However, people's thinking, when it comes to service, has not changed. The customer never really had the choice of more or less service. It was just taken away.

The business that still provides additional service for the same cost has an advantage over competitors that do not. After all, isn't that the point? You can become an outstanding salesperson! It's true. When you extend yourself to the customer just a little extra, the word gets around. Being helpful and accommodating to your customer costs nothing but a little extra time and effort. Increased sales are the result.

In our fast-paced world, an act of kindness or even common courtesy, throws people off guard. Your mother's admonition to "mind your manners" is especially relevant in today's business environment.

With the advent of the global marketplace, sales protocol not only crosses geographic boundaries, but also cultural ones. We must present our best self not only to our colleagues, neighbors and friends, but also to the world if we are to remain a player in the global economy.

Vanishing Peddler

Selling methods advance with time. Years ago, the peddler would arrive with his wagon, and once situated in the town square, begin to "hawk," or sell, his wares. These "salesmen" of the past were the dentist, the evangelist, the doctor, the druggist, and many others. Their goods and services were as varied as their professions.

As people moved from rural areas to towns, the old peddlers evolved into door-to-door salesmen. They established routes and customers, but the goods they offered were much the same. In their trunks were an array of items including tea, coffee, household items and medicine. The doctor even made house calls.

There were two kinds of peddlers and door-to-door delivery men—honest and dishonest. As the crooked peddler was run out of town, his counterpart, the dishonest door to door salesman was shut out once and for all.

Products and services are no longer sold from a wagon or at the door, but they are still sold. In my estimation, the sales rep will always have a job. People want the personal interaction that exists between buyer and seller.

High Tech Advances

Goods and services are sold differently today than in the past, but the sale still consists of two main players—the buyer and the seller. Regardless of how technologically complex our society becomes, the sale is simply between the buyer and the seller.

For example, the most sophisticated computer in the world may be designed. If something goes wrong with the software program, the operator may seek "support." This support will be provided by a human being. The fact remains, people operate the machine. People think; machines do not.

Telecommunication technology advances daily. Many companies and individuals "surf the Net" sharing information and selling their products. Fax machines have eliminated some of the mailman's burden. Bank withdrawals are easy and convenient with automatic teller machines, but with the advent of electronic transfer, even ATMs will soon be a thing of the past.

Electronic communication advances at an unbelievable rate. News printed on paper may soon be collected only for its curiosity value. It's already predicted that images, in addition to voice, will be transmitted by telephone.

Vehicles will become safer due to accident prevention devices. Space barriers will electronically prevent automobiles from colliding with each other. Airplanes will have crash-proof compartments, and ships that sink will be tragedies of the past. Because of these advances, travel will be safer in the twenty-first century. Technology will continue to make what is conceivable a reality.

Surviving Sales Reps

With all my guessing about the future, one matter remains. It has to do with what it takes for a salesperson to survive. It will continue to take three characteristics: honesty, knowledge, and the ability to communicate the first two to the customer.

Honesty is an individual choice. You can decide to be honest or dishonest. However, if you are going to be a successful sales representative, there is no choice. Salespeople must be trustworthy.

Along with integrity, sales representatives need to be knowledgeable. Information and experience used positively will add to any sales career. Simply put, a salesperson must know his or her product. Competence and sincerity are the two main ingredients for successful salespeople. The more difficult undertaking is the job of convincing your customer that you own both qualities.

I wanted to share with you what many have shared with me. This is why I decided to write this book. I do not take credit for what is written here. Instead I choose to share whatever credit is due with all the salesmen and women with whom I have crossed paths: I have learned from each and every one. The buyers taught me not only to be grateful, but to be proud of my chosen profession. I am a salesman, and I offer to you what others have offered me: sales knowledge and its application. The honesty required is your commitment to the profession.

Summary

Section 10:

Twentieth Century and Beyond

- Extend yourself to the customer. Increased sales are the result of outstanding service.

- The sales representative is part of the selling process.

- Technology is of great value but remember, people think, machines don't.

- For a sales rep to be successful it takes three characteristics: honesty, knowledge, and the ability to communicate the first two to the customer.

INDEX

174

175

N

O

P

Q

R

177